Money Around the World

Earning Money

Rebecca Rissman

Heinemann Library
Chicago, Illinois

Designed by Joanna Hinton-Malivoire
Photo Research by Tracy Cummins and Heather Mauldin
Printed in China by South China Printing Company Limited

12 11 10 09 08
10 9 8 7 6 5 4 3 2 1

The Library of Congress has cataloged the first edition as follows:
Rissman, Rebecca.
 Earning money / Rebecca Rissman.
     p. cm. -- (Money around the world)
 Includes bibliographical references and index.
 ISBN-13: 978-1-4329-1069-3 (hc)
 ISBN-13: 978-1-4329-1074-7 (pb)
 1. Vocational guidance--Juvenile literature. 2. Occupations--Juvenile literature. 3. Wages--Juvenile literature. I. Title.
 HF5381.2.R54 2008
 331.702--dc22
                            2007035623

Acknowledgments
The author and publisher are grateful to the following for permission to reproduce copyright material: ©Alamy p. **19** (Peter Titmuss), ©Corbis pp. **17** (Stock This Way/Hill Street Studios), **18** (Atlantide Phototravel); **p.16** ©drr.net (Keith Dennemiller); ©Getty Images pp. **4** (Bruce Forster), **6** (Andrew Hetherington), **7** (Zubin Shroff), **9** (Gavin Hellier), **10** (Michael Blann), **11** (Cancan Chu), **14** (Margo Silver), **15** (Jose Luis Pelaez Inc.), **23a** (Bruce Forster); ©Masterfile p. **12** (Jerzyworks); ©PeterArnold Inc. pp. **13** (Martin Harvey), **20** (JORGEN SCHYTTE); ©The World Bank pp. **5**, **23b** (Eric Miller), **8**, **21** (Curt Carnemark).

Cover photograph reproduced with permission of ©Alamy (Jon Arnold Images).
Back cover photograph reproduced with the permission of The World Bank/Curt Carnemark.

Every effort has been made to contact copyright holders of any material reproduced in this book. Any omissions will be rectified in subsequent printings if notice is given to the publisher.

Contents

Earning Money

People work to earn money.

People work at jobs.

People are paid for work.

People are paid money.

Goods

People sell goods to earn money.

Goods are things we eat.

Goods are things we use.

People sell bread to earn money.

People sell fruit to earn money.

People sell houses to earn money.

People sell pots to earn money.

Services

People sell services to earn money.

Services are jobs people do for others.

People make food to earn money.

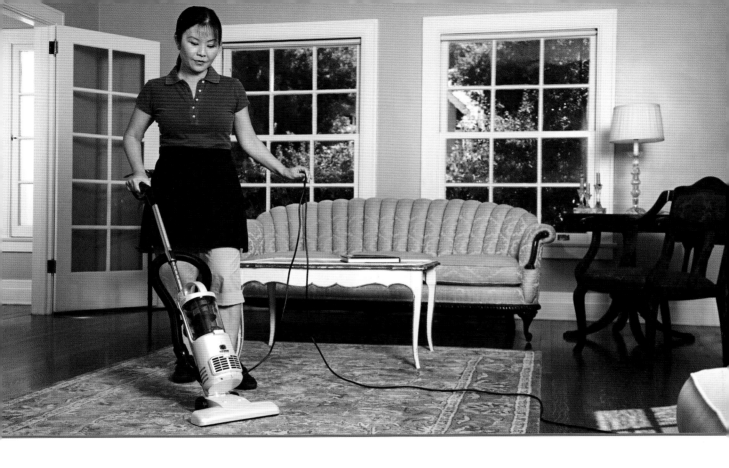

People clean homes to earn money.

People drive buses to earn money.

People deliver mail to earn money.

Money Around the World

People earn money around
the world.

People work at jobs around the world.

Goods and Services

goods
- fruit
- clothing
- toys
- dvds
- books

services
- giving a haircut
- babysitting
- serving food
- driving a bus
- cleaning a house

Picture Glossary

earn to get money for work you have done

work what people do to earn money. People work at jobs.

Index

Note to Parents and Teachers
Before reading: Ask children if they have ever earned money with a garage sale or lemonade stand. Ask them what the word "work" means, and to name different types of jobs.

After reading: Discuss with children that people work at jobs so that they can earn money. Help children distinguish between goods and services by drawing a chart and placing appropriate jobs in each category.